Global Connections

ACTION *literacy*

Carmel Reilly

Global Connections
ISBN 978-0-86431-550-2

Written by Carmel Reilly
First published 2007
by ACER Press
Australian Council *for* Educational Research Ltd
19 Prospect Hill Road, Camberwell, Victoria 3124
Copyright © 2007 Australian Council *for* Educational Research Ltd

Action Literacy and Action Numeracy program developed by

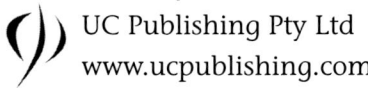 UC Publishing Pty Ltd
www.ucpublishing.com

Edited by Kerry Nagle
Designed by Rachel De Luca
Cover photograph: Rob Friedman
Illustrations: James Hart pp. 5, 8, 9, 11, 26, 30; all other illustrations UC Publishing.
Photo credits: iStockphoto pp. 4, 6, 7, 10, 11, 12, 13b, 15, 17, 19a, 24, 25, 29, 31; Newspix pp.16, 18, 19b; UC Publishing p. 23.

Printed by Craft Print International Ltd

contents

Everything is connected

In today's world, everyone and everything is connected. It is easy and quick to travel from one side of the world to another by plane. News is beamed from country to country by satellite. People can talk to each other over long distances by phone or on the Internet.

Australians often feel that they are a long way from the rest of the world. But even when we stay at home, we see many reminders of other cultures. Much of our food, clothing, entertainment and news comes from overseas. A lot of the goods and equipment we use are designed and made overseas.

However, not everything goes in one direction. Many products designed and made in Australia are used by people in other countries. Australian culture is known worldwide. The work of Australian artists, musicians, actors, sports people and entertainers is seen by many people in other countries.

Look at this Australian family, the Kavans.

This is the Kavan family

Mum, Dad, Miah (12) and Sam (10)

Like most Australians, the Kavans have all kinds of global connections. From when they wake up in the morning to when they go to sleep at night, they use and see things that have come from all over the world.

This is a day in their lives.

8.00 a.m.
Starting the day

It's Saturday. Miah wakes up to the sound of a rap song blaring from her radio alarm clock. She crawls out of bed and stretches. She pulls on her Chinese silk dressing gown over her Indian cotton pyjamas.

Radio alarm clocks

Radio alarm clocks were first developed in the 1950s. Although they are designed and marketed by companies all over the world, most are manfactured in China.

Rap music

Rap music began in New York in the 1970s. When African-American DJs played records at parties, they would often talk along to parts of the music. This talking was known as rapping. Now rap music is made and played by all kinds of people all around the world.

Pyjamas

The word pyjama comes from Urdu, a language spoken in Pakistan and India. *Pay* is the Urdu word for leg and *jama* means clothing.

In the room next door, Sam is half-awake. He pulls his Hungarian goose feather quilt up over his head and tries to go back to sleep.

Ten minutes later, Mum comes in and wakes Sam again.

"Time to get up, Sam. We've got lots to do today. You've got a soccer game and we're going to that multicultural festival later on."

Saturday 12 October

9.30	Soccer against White St Primary School
11.30	Multicultural Festival at Seddon Park
5.00	Help Dad to get the BBQ and tables ready
6.30	Patels here for BBQ

The FIFA World Cup

The FIFA (Federation of International Football Associations) World Cup is the most important event in men's soccer. The cup is played every four years in a different country. In 2006 it was held in Germany and in 2010 it will be held in South Africa. The winner of the last World Cup was Italy.

Teams representing countries from all over the world compete for the cup. The World Cup is the most watched sporting event in the world. Hundreds of thousands of people flock to the games themselves. More than a billion people watch the event on television and the Internet.

8.10 a.m.
Breakfast

The Kavan family sit down to a hearty breakfast. Soon they will set off to play and watch sport for the morning. They're eating the sort of breakfast that many Australian families might eat on the weekend. However, a lot of the food, and the ingredients themselves, come from countries all around the globe.

1. Buckwheat pancakes
2. Maple syrup
3. Kiwi fruit
4. Milk
5. Orange juice
6. Tea
7. Coffee
8. Cups/plates
9. Glassware
10. Cutlery

1. USA
2. Canada
3. New Zealand
4. Australia
5. Australia
6. Sri Lanka
7. Papua New Guinea
8. England
9. France
10. Korea

8.30 a.m.
News of the day

The Kavan parents enjoy relaxing over breakfast. As they finish their coffee and tea, they like to read the newspaper. They like to find out what is happening in the world.

A hundred years ago, there were no planes, radios or satellites. News travelled slowly. It could take weeks, even months, for news to travel from Europe to Australia.

Now news can be sent almost instantly around the world. People in Australia receive news from overseas on their radios, TVs and the Internet only minutes after an event happens. They can even have it downloaded to their mobile phone.

After breakfast, the Kavan children watch TV in the family room while their parents read the Saturday papers. They often pick up bits and pieces of the news from the radio, TV or the Internet.

"Mum! Look! They've found a new kind of snake in Japan," says Sam, pointing at the TV. "It looks amazing."

Television was not invented by just one person. It was developed over many years by a number of scientists, mostly in the United Kingdom and the USA. The first public television broadcast was made in the USA in 1934. However, the first television broadcast in Australia was not until 1956.

It takes longer to print and deliver whole newspapers than it does to put together a news story for TV. However, newspapers often have a lot more in-depth information about each story. Newspapers are also good because they are easy to carry around. They can be read anywhere.

The Daily News

NEW SNAKE FOUND IN JAPAN

A new species of snake has been found on Kyushu, Japan's southern-most island.

A local farmer, Mr Ken Obu, found the snake as he was tending to his vegetable garden last week. He noticed its unusual green and red markings. Mr Obu, who is used to handling snakes, captured the animal and called the authorities.

Experts from Tokyo Zoo flew to Kyushu and examined the snake. They believe the find represents a breakthrough in the study of snakes. They think this particular snake is related to a new species recently found in the north-west of Australia, named the Red-eared Green Belly.

The area where the new snake was found on Kyushu

FROM THE NEWS TO YOU

Newspaper journalists go back to the newsroom to write up their stories and process their photos. If they are a long way away from the newsroom, they can phone in their stories or send them by email. Photos can be sent digitally as well. At the newsroom, editors read the story. They sometimes make changes or cut it back if it is too long. Once the story is edited, it is ready to be typeset with all the other stories in the paper. After typesetting, the paper is printed. The printed copies are then sent to newsagents.

A printer at work

FROM CARRIER PIGEONS TO THE INTERNET

Reuters is a famous international news service. It has a staff of more than 15 000 people working in 89 countries. Every day, the staff gathers news that is sent to places all around the world. Reuters was started in London in 1851 by Paul Julius Reuter.

Reuter had come from Germany where he had run a local news service using carrier pigeons!

Over the years that followed, the Reuters service always used the newest technology. It used radio technology in the 1920s. In the 1960s, it made its first satellite news report. In the 1970s, Reuters journalists began to use computers to write and send stories between their agencies. In recent times, Reuters was the first to use instant video imaging.

After breakfast, the Kavan family drive to the sports grounds. Miah plays tennis here and Sam plays soccer.

Transport plays a big part in modern life. Like most people, the Kavans need cars, trains or buses to get to school and to work. Without a car, the Kavans would probably not be able to get to the sports ground on Saturdays.

Other transport

Transport does not just carry people from place to place. It also moves goods around the world. If countries are connected by land, the goods can be carried in trucks and on trains. If countries are a long way away from each other, many goods will have to be sent by air or by sea.

Most goods sent by sea travel on container ships. Containers are huge metal boxes, about the size of a large truck. Some modern container ships can carry as many as 15 000 containers. These can contain anything from engine parts, to toys, to furniture.

Another important product transported by sea is oil. Oil is carried in huge ships called oil tankers. There can be thousands of container ships and oil tankers sailing around the world at any one time.

New technologies also help in transporting goods. Information about products can be recorded in computers. This helps people to keep track of them and make sure that they arrive safely at their destination. Better navigation and communication equipment means that ships can be warned about storms at sea so that they can take different routes. Better loading and unloading equipment at ports makes it quicker and easier to get goods on and off ships.

Footballs made in Pakistan

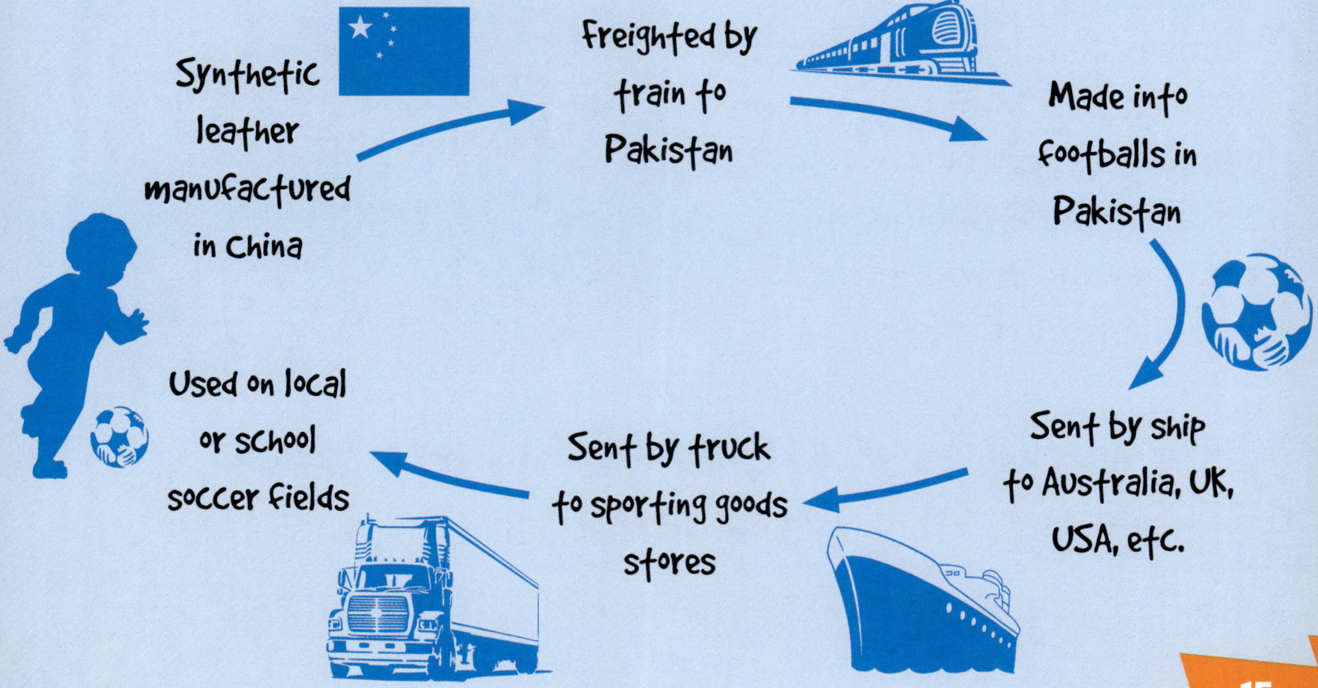

Synthetic leather manufactured in China

Freighted by train to Pakistan

Made into footballs in Pakistan

Sent by ship to Australia, UK, USA, etc.

Sent by truck to sporting goods stores

Used on local or school soccer fields

Each weekend, hundreds of thousands of children around the country play sport or take sporting lessons. The children play sport locally but the sports they play come from all over the world.

Tennis

Tennis was played in France from the 11th or 12th century onwards. In the late 1800s, the English took up the game but changed it. They moved it outdoors and used racquets instead of their hands to hit the ball. Australia was one of the first countries to take up playing the modern game of tennis in the early 20th century. Many Australian tennis players, such as Rod Laver, Evonne Goolagong and Lleyton Hewitt, have become world famous.

The name tennis comes from the French term "tenez!" or "take this!" This was shouted out by the French royal tennis players just before they were about to serve.

Basketball

Basketball was invented in the USA in 1891 by a Canadian teacher, James Naismith. At the time, all the winter sports were played outdoors. But Naismith's school wanted a game that people could play indoors so they didn't have to worry about the weather.

Within a few years basketball became a sport played all around the USA. In 1936 it was included as an Olympic sport. Today it is played in countries all around the world.

The American National Basketball Association (NBA) is the largest basketball association in the world. Players come from all around the world to join one of the 30 NBA teams. At the beginning of 2006, there were 82 non-American players from 38 countries playing in the NBA. Three of those players were from Australia.

Australian Rules football

In Melbourne in 1857, Tom Wills and three friends decided to create a new football game that would help to keep them fit in winter. This game was known as Australian Rules football. Most people think that Wills and his friends based the game on Rugby, with some influences from Gaelic (Irish) football. It might also have been influenced by a local Aboriginal ball game called Marn Grook.

Australian Rules football quickly became popular in Victoria, and then the rest of the states. Today, Australian Rules football is played and watched more than any other football code in Australia. Since the 1980s, Australian Rules football has also been taken up by small groups of local players in countries such as Japan, Sweden and the United States.

International sporting events

Sporting events have always brought people together. Television coverage allows millions of people all around the world to see sporting competitions from every part of the globe.

Swimming

People have been swimming since prehistoric times, but it was only since the 1800s that people became interested in swimming as a sport. Swimming was one of the sports in the first Olympics in 1896. However, women were not allowed to compete in Olympic swimming until 1912.

A world swimming championship is held every two years. Australia has always had strong swimmers. Many have been world record holders and Olympic medal winners, such as Dawn Fraser, Murray Rose, Shane Gould, Kieren Perkins and Ian Thorpe, to name just a few.

Leisel Jones won a gold medal in the FINA World Swimming Championships in 2007.

Manufacturing sporting goods

Australia's main supplier of sporting goods is China. Other countries that manufacture sporting goods, like balls and nets, are Taiwan, Hong Kong, Vietnam, Pakistan and India.

11.30 a.m. off to the festival

After the Kavan children finish their sports, their parents take them to a local festival. The "Let's Celebrate Australia" festival is a special event held once a year in their town. It celebrates multiculturalism and cultural diversity. The Kavans have come along to the festival to find out more about the people who live in the local community. They've also come to have fun for the afternoon.

LET'S CELEBRATE AUSTRALIA

Tent A

Stage 1

Stage 2

MORNING PROGRAMME

10.00 Official welcome from the city council and the traditional owners of the land.

10.00–5.00 Art and craft stalls

10.00–5.00 Food stalls

11.00 A workshop on traditional Balinese carving will be held in Tent A

12.00 A Chinese dragon display will be held on the lawn in front of Stage 2

12.30 An introduction to the didgeridoo will be held on Stage 1

1.00 Balinese dancers will perform at the Main Stage

2.00 Storytelling in Tent A

2.30 A film will be shown about the building of the Taj Mahal in India in Tent B

3.00 Music and dance demonstrations

Australia is made up of people from a wide variety of countries and ethnic groups.

Many people in the population have British and Irish backgrounds. There are also groups of people from Europe, Asia, the Pacific, North and South America and Africa as well as Aboriginal peoples and Torres Strait Islanders.

The Chinese Community

The Chinese are one of Australia's oldest migrant groups. Large numbers of Chinese men came here in the mid 19th century during the Gold Rush.

Today, Chinese people make up the fifth largest ethnic group living in Australia. Chinatowns can be found in most of Australia's cities where people can buy Chinese groceries and eat Chinese food.

Chinese New Year is popular for all of the community.

The Sudanese Community

The Sudanese community is one of the newest communities in Australia. Many Sudanese people have arrived in the last twenty years. They have come to escape the civil war which has been fought in their country since the early 1980s. They are the fifth largest migrant group to arrive in Australia over the last few years.

12.00 noon Lunchtime!

Australia today is home to people from hundreds of different cultures and each culture has its own special foods. Community festivals are good places to sample many of the different kinds of foods that are available.

One of the most popular things at the "Let's Celebrate Australia" festival is the wonderful variety of food. Delicious treats from many different countries are on offer. The Kavans love sampling food they have never eaten before. They also enjoy eating old favourites.

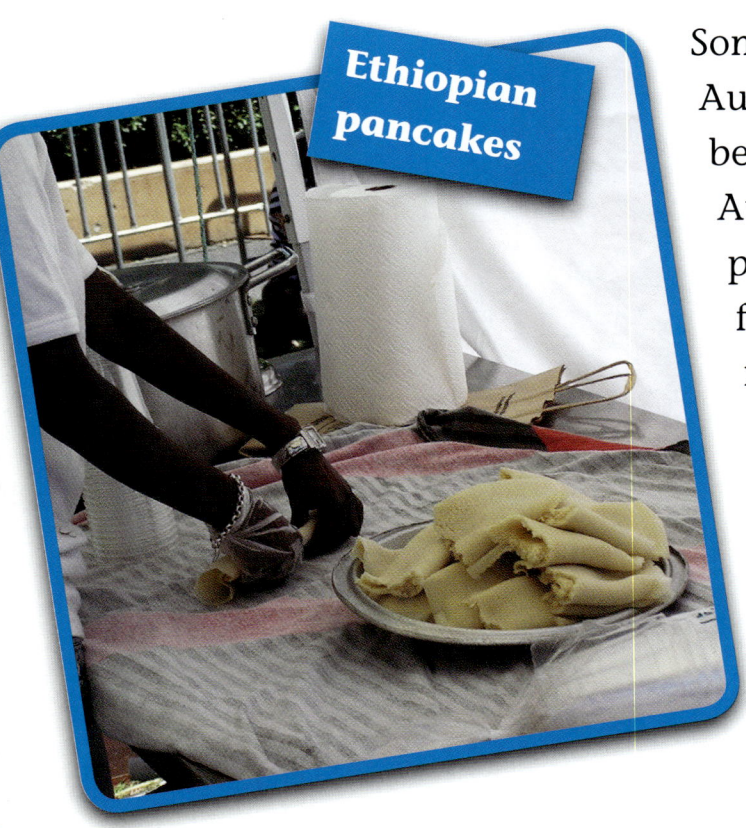

Ethiopian pancakes

Some of the foods brought to Australia by migrants have become an everyday part of Australian cooking. Many people make the Italian favourites of pasta and risotto at home. Chinese dishes like stir-fries and fried rice are also very popular. Indian, Thai and Japanese restaurants have sprung up in cities and large towns across Australia.

Kebabs

German sausages

Italian doughnuts

Soup and satays

Most of us begin to get to know about other cultures from their food and their arts and crafts. At the festival, there are stalls displaying craftwork, art and furniture. These come from countries as varied as India, China, Egypt, Chile and Papua New Guinea.

Mum and Miah stop to admire the display from Indonesia. Indonesia is famous for its beautiful materials and wood carving.

"These are beautiful," says Miah, picking out a batik sarong.

"I love these chairs," says Mum. "When we went to Bali, there were chairs like this at the house where we stayed in the hills."

- Indonesia is one of Australia's nearest neighbours.

- It is home to 246 million people with many different cultures and religions.

- Indonesia has the fourth largest population of any country in the world.

- The Indonesian language is taught in many Australian schools.

- Bali is just one of the more than 17 000 islands that make up Indonesia. Hundreds of thousands of tourists visit Bali each year.

Bali

2.00 p.m.
Storytelling time

The Kavan children go to the storytelling tent to listen to some traditional folktales from other countries. The theme of the stories today is "How people were created".

Folktales are stories that are very old and have been handed down from generation to generation. The stories often explained things about the world and passed on information and wisdom. Folktales include legends and traditions, fairytales, animal tales, fables, and myths. Before writing, folktales were told orally. Later, many stories were written down.

A Maori traditional tale

How the first people were created

In Maori myth, Rangi (the sky father) and Papa (the Earth mother) came from the great darkness and created the heavens and the Earth. Between them, they had a number of sons who became gods. One of these was Tane (pronounced *Tar-nay*), god of forests.

After living on the Earth for many years, Tane started to feel lonely. Although he had brothers, he wanted someone special to spend his time with. He wanted to have a mate and a family of his own. Because he was a god, Tane realised that he could create a being himself. He went down to the beach and made a figure out of a mound of sand. He bent down and breathed life into the figure. It got up and started to move around. Tane had created the very first human being—a woman. He called her Hine-ahu-one (pronounced *Hee-nay-ah-hoo-oh-nay*) and she became his wife.

Tane and Hine-ahu-one had children, and their offspring covered the Earth. But there was a big difference between the gods and humans. When Tane breathed life into Hine-ahu-one, it meant that one day the life breath would leave her and she would die. And so it was that all the offspring of Tane and Hine-ahu-one were humans like their mother and, unlike the gods, they could not live forever.

3.00 p.m. Music and dance

After the storytelling is over, the Kavan family all go to the main stage to watch a display of music and dance. Every culture has developed its own music, dance and performance. Many songs and dances tell stories or celebrate special events. They can be important ways of passing on the history and beliefs of a society.

There are thousands of different folk dances throughout Turkey.

Cook Islander musicians play traditional drums.

Morrismen perform traditional English folk dances in costume.

The Chinese dragon master demonstrates how to manage a Chinese dragon.

Australian Indigenous art, music and culture is known all over the world. The musical instrument, the didgeridoo, is a good example of a part of Aboriginal culture that is known everywhere.

Didgeridoos have been played by Indigenous northern Australians for thousands of years. They are made by hollowing out small tree trunks, which are then decorated in traditional tribal styles. Didgeridoos, as well as clap sticks, are usually played at special tribal ceremonies, alongside traditional singing and dancing.

5.30 p.m.
A relaxing end to the day

After spending most of the afternoon at the fair, the Kavans head home.

Tonight, they are having a barbecue with their new neighbours—Mrs Patel and her son Ravi. They migrated from India two years ago. Ravi and Sam are in the same class at school.

The Kavans make some salads and fire up the barbecue.
The Patels arrive at 6.30 with some Indian snacks and sweets.

In 2006, more than 11 000 people migrated from India to Australia. This makes Indians the third largest migrant group after people from Britain and New Zealand.

"Are you enjoying living in Australia?" Mum asks Mrs Patel over dinner.

Mrs Patel smiles. "Oh yes. The cultures are very different and that has been hard to get used to sometimes. But people have been very kind and we have made some good friends here."

After the Patels leave, Miah, Sam, Mum and Dad clean up. Then, the family sit down to watch a documentary about Tanzania on TV.

"This is about the place where our sponsored child lives," says Mum.

"When I get older, I'd like to help people in poorer countries," says Sam.

"How do you think you could do that?" asks Dad.

"I'm not sure yet," replies Sam. "But I know I'll find some way."

Tanzania is in east Africa. It is home to over 37 million people.

Index